Theo von Taane

# Basketball 2 in 1 Tacticboard & Training Workbook

The 2 in 1 Tacticboard & Training Workbook for fast creation of coaching instructions/game tactics and schemes, doesn't only offer sport specific preprints (playing field and space for notes), but also a cover, usable as a dry erase panel (whiteboard pen is needed).

ADVANTAGES:
- notebook with sport specific preprints (playing field) for fast and simple sketching of coaching instructions/game tactics and schemes

- If all pages of the notebook are used, the cover is still a dry erase panel (tacticboard)

- Due to a handy format, the notebook can be comfortably used in any situation (e.g. on the way or on the playing field)

- Perfect for spontaneous collection of ideas or as a memorization tool

- Practical handling due to easy pocket format

*Bibliografische Information der Deutschen Nationalbibliothek:*
*Die Deutsche Nationalbibliothek verzeichnet diese Publikation in der Deutschen Nationalbibliografie; detaillierte bibliografische Daten sind im Internet über http://dnb.dnb.de abrufbar.*

© *2016 Theo von Taane; 2. Auflage*

*Texte und Illustrationen:* **Theo von Taane**

*Herstellung und Verlag: BoD – Books on Demand, Norderstedt*

*ISBN: 9783734749681*

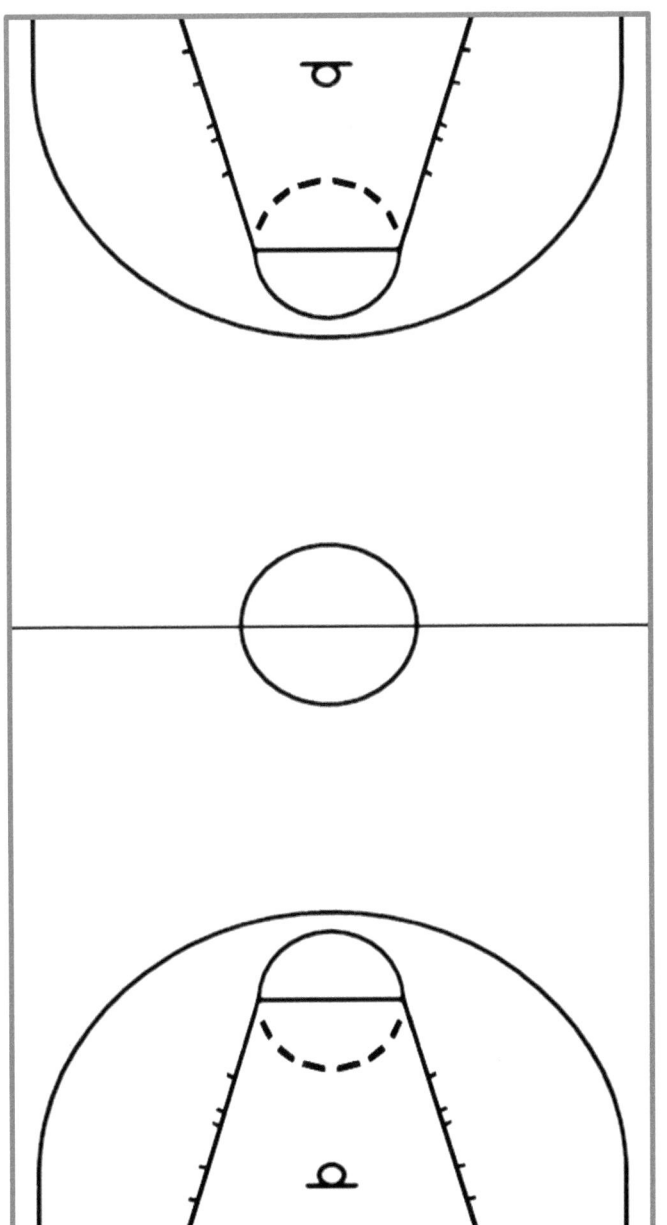

# Books of Theo von Taane

| book | ISBN / order nr. |
|---|---|
| Football Tacticboard & Training Workbook | 9783734749605 |
| Badminton Tacticboard & Training Workbook | 9783734749643 |
| Baseball Tacticboard & Training Workbook | 9783734749650 |
| Basketball Tacticboard & Training Workbook | 9783734749681 |
| Bowling Tacticboard & Training Workbook | 9783734749698 |
| Cricket Tacticboard & Training Workbook | 9783734749711 |
| Ice Hockey Tacticboard & Training Workbook | 9783734749728 |
| Fencing Tacticboard & Training Workbook | 9783734749735 |
| Field Hockey Tacticboard & Training Workbook | 9783734749810 |
| Football (Soccer) Tacticboard & Training Workbook | 9783734749827 |
| Futsal Tacticboard & Training Workbook | 9783734749834 |
| Handball Tacticboard & Training Workbook | 9783734749841 |
| Lacrosse Women Tacticboard & Training Workbook | 9783734749858 |
| Lacrosse Men Tacticboard & Training Workbook | 9783734749865 |
| Netball Tacticboard & Training Workbook | 9783734749872 |
| Rugby Tacticboard & Training Workbook | 9783734749889 |
| Chess Tacticboard & Training Workbook | 9783734749896 |
| Squash Tacticboard & Training Workbook | 9783734749902 |
| Tennis Tacticboard & Training Workbook | 9783734749919 |
| Table Tennis Tacticboard & Training Workbook | 9783734749926 |
| Volleyball Tacticboard & Training Workbook | 9783734749933 |
| Water Polo Tacticboard & Training Workbook | 9783734749940 |

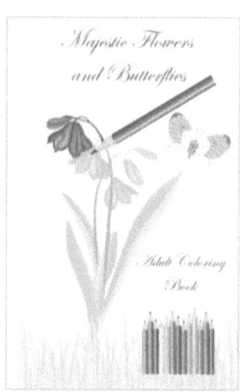

### Majestic Flowers and Butterflies
- Adult Coloring Book - ISBN: 9783739227085

This coloring book for adults contains 36 beautiful patterns of various flowers. Experience hours full of stress relief, mindful calm, creative expression and fun.

Use crayons, felt-tip pens and colored pencils to give the patterns a personal touch.

Millions of people worldwide have rediscovered the simple relaxation and joy of coloring!

Join this community and find yourself enchanted by the magical passion of inspiring coloring.